The Lands and Peoples Series

CANADA

The Lands and Peoples Series

MOUNT ROBSON, IN THE ROCKY MOUNTAINS

THE LANDS AND PEOPLES SERIES

CANADA

by

R. L. GORDON

WITH FOUR PLATES IN COLOUR
ELEVEN PHOTOGRAPHS AND A MAP

NEW YORK
THE MACMILLAN COMPANY

J
971
G

5-11-60

MADE AND PRINTED IN GREAT BRITAIN BY
MORRISON AND GIBB LIMITED, LONDON AND EDINBURGH

CONTENTS

ILLUSTRATIONS

These four plates in colour are from photographs by the late Frank S. Smythe, reproduced by kind permission of Mrs. Frank Smythe.

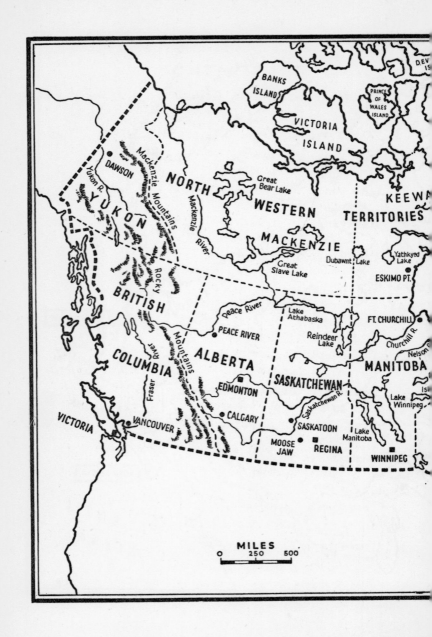

FROM COD TO SALMON

RUMBLING into Edinburgh after a sleepless night sitting up in a third-class compartment, you feel you have come a very long way since you left London the night before. And in fact you have travelled a good part of the length of the Island. To a Canadian or an American such a journey would seem as nothing compared with the journeys he is accustomed to make in his own country. To cross from Halifax on the Atlantic coast to Vancouver on the edge of the Pacific takes him five full days of train travel. The most difficult idea for a visitor to grasp is the size of Canada. You may take him to the shores of lakes so vast that they are more like oceans than lakes: into Lake Superior, with an area of 31,820 square miles, Ireland would fit very comfortably with something like 5,000 square miles to spare. You may point out to him that England and Wales would fit into Canada some seventy-five times and still leave room around the edges. If you wish to startle him with facts and figures you may even tell him that the area of this huge country is nearly 4,000,000 square miles, but he will still have only a very imperfect idea of how big the land really is. Over all this great stretch of earth, rock, forest, and ice, there are not many more people than in the combined populations of London and Glasgow.

Canada is too big to put between the covers of this book. Between the fisherman catching cod on

the Atlantic and his brother catching salmon on
the Pacific there are thousands of miles of different
types of country and some millions of different
types of people. There are a few large cities and
many small towns, villages, and lonely settlements.
There is in fact as much variety across the face
of Canada in country, climate, industry, people,
and the way of life as its size would suggest. We
can see only a little here, but there is much that
must be left for the reader to see for himself when
he comes.

We can speak of Canada more conveniently
first of all by regions—the Maritimes, French
Canada, Ontario, and "The West".   Roughly
speaking the country was explored and settled from
east to west—with vast stretches of the Northland
still empty and unexplored to-day—logically, therefore, we should carry out our exploration in the
same direction. Having discovered then something
about the geography, history, and people of the
various sections of the country; having formed some
idea of what Canada "is like", we shall look at
some other sides of Canadian life.

The visitor to Canada must try to understand
one other thing about the country besides its size,
and that is its age. This land is very young. Britain,
and indeed all of Europe, was already old when
the first English and French settlers were chopping
trees for their Canadian cabins and trading muskets
for a pile of beaver pelts. In many ways Canada
has grown up quickly. In government, in industry,
in what we call "standard of living" the country
has come to manhood in a remarkably short time.
In other ways Canada is still a schoolboy with

something of a schoolboy's inexperience and, more important, with much of a schoolboy's enthusiasm for life and eagerness for what the future may bring.

The history of Canada does not go back very far. There are still men living who can tell you from first hand knowledge much of the history of their part of the country. There are no truly ancient traditions, no Gothic or Norman cathedrals, and the nearest approach to the ancient castles of Europe are a few of the original Hudson's Bay Company forts which still remain standing. But if Canada is poorer because of this lack of ties with the distant past, she is rich in something else—richer than many of her older sisters—rich in the fact that she is still making her own traditions, still looking for and finding answers to the many problems which lie in the future. Canada cannot look very far behind but she looks a long way ahead.

THE MARITIMES

THE four provinces on the east coast of Canada are called "The Maritimes": New Brunswick, Nova Scotia, Prince Edward Island, and Newfoundland. Of these, Nova Scotia, tracing its birth back to the Royal Charter of New Scotland granted more than three hundred years ago, was the first colony of Great Britain to possess its own flag. Only five years after Columbus made his first voyage of discovery, John Cabot reached the north coast of Nova Scotia, now called Cape Breton Island, and took possession of the land for King Henry VII. It was summer; the weather was warm; the soil was rich and fertile; and the vegetation lush and green. Cabot believed he had reached Asia and looked forward to returning with a cargo of silks, spices, and precious stones. But the rocky shores of this proud province may well have seen white men some five or six hundred years before Cabot's brave expedition.

An Icelandic saga tells of the founding of a colony in Greenland in the year 980 by Eric-the-Red, and of how, not long after, his son, Leif-the-Lucky, in a small ship and with a crew of thirty-five good Norsemen set off south and west across the untravelled sea. At length he and his men saw ahead a bleak and desolate stretch of coast, a coast of rock and snow. They named this new country Helluland. Southward still they sailed until they came to a spacious wooded country of wide, sandy

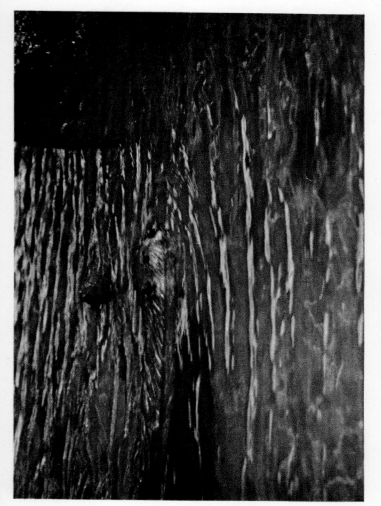

BEAVER SWIMMING IN AN ALBERTA LAKE

beaches sloping down to the sea. Following along the coast they reached at last an island lying on the north side of this land at the mouth of a bay. The weather was wild and stormy. Leif and his men sailed up the bay to a river and up the river, towing their boat, to a lake. On the shores of that lake they made their shelters and passed the winter in the wilderness of this unknown and unnamed land. Here in the autumn and the following summer they found wild grapes growing in abundance and they called the country Vinland. Before winter came again the party set off once more for the Greenland colony with some lumber and grapes and tales of adventure and endurance for the winter evenings. Where was Vinland? That question has never been answered with complete certainty, but all true "Maritimers" know that it was either Chaleur Bay in the northern part of what is now the Province of New Brunswick, or some bay on the coast of Nova Scotia. Whether or not these hardy voyagers left some of their number to found a colony we do not know. If any settlement were made it was left to the mercies of the barbaric Micmac Indians and no relics have been found. There is a sword, however, a short Icelandic sword which may be seen in the Ontario Museum in Toronto. It was found in 1937 near Beardmore, Ontario. Whether it was traded with the Indians on the east coast and then by them with interior tribes, or whether the Norsemen found their way much farther into this country than has ever been supposed, is another question which remains unanswered.

Canada is a new country, but in Nova Scotia one

is much more aware of the past than anywhere else across the country except, perhaps, for parts of Quebec. New Brunswick, which was once a part of Nova Scotia, shares its links with the past. The history of these neighbour provinces, lands of lakes and forest, is, like that of so much of Eastern Canada, a long tale of bitter French and English rivalry. Under the French the territory was known as Acadie, anglicised later to Acadia. Following in Cabot's wake came the Portuguese navigator, Real, and a Florentine with the wonderful name, Giovanni Da Verrazano, who claimed the coast for France. It was Jacques Cartier, however, who really laid the foundations of New France in North America. The Portuguese soon faded out of the scene and the rivalry between France and England was born. We shall have more to say of this rivalry, which is not completely dead even to-day, when we come to talk later of French Canada—of what is now the Province of Quebec. The French Period in the Maritimes, with its pioneer hardships, its tales of fur trading ventures, of starvation, of brutal Indian warfare and of the endless struggles with the English, makes a stirring story.

Of the two remaining provinces Prince Edward Island is the smallest and Newfoundland is the newest in Canada. Although she is the youngest of the provinces she was the oldest of all British colonies. Newfoundlanders have always led a hard life on their rugged and rock-bound island. Sir Humphrey Gilbert, standing on a hill overlooking the now famous harbour of St. John's, read aloud to the crews of his four ships and as many members of the foreign ships in the bay as he could persuade to attend, the commission entrusted to him and formally claimed possession of the country for Queen Elizabeth. Another Elizabeth, only a short time before she too was to become Queen, left North America for England from the same harbour. From the beginning Newfoundland has lived by the products of the sea. Her men have put forth in their boats year after year; their sons and their sons' sons still follow that tradition. For more than a century before the establishment of French or English colonies in North America, the fishermen of Western Europe came year after year to Newfoundland to fill their boats with cod for the markets of the Old World. It is a lucky boy to-day who has survived his childhood without suffering doses of Newfoundland's cod-liver oil.

The province has never been wealthy. In the early "nineteen-thirties" with a quarter of the island's population without work or money and the situation rapidly growing worse, Newfoundland was obliged to ask Britain for help. A Commission of Government was set up and, by mutual agreement, Newfoundland self-government was temporarily suspended until such a time as the country could once more be self-supporting. In 1948 Newfoundland voted to become Canada's tenth province.

Prince Edward Island is not only the smallest province in Canada; it is the most densely populated. In the whole of Canada there are, on an average, only four people to the square mile. In Prince Edward Island there are forty. (In England and Wales there are seven hundred and fifty-three people to the square mile.) Unlike its

big sister Nova Scotia, Prince Edward Island is a
a land of agriculture. Its beaches are broad and
sandy; its land fertile and rolling. It is a "green
and pleasant" garden province.

To-day, as in the past, the "Maritimers" live
by the sea. There have been, and there are, other
industries and other interests but, like the British,
the "Maritimers" are a seafaring people. When
the sloop-of-war *Sphinx* led thirteen ships containing
2,576 colonists into the bay known as Chebucto
Harbour, Halifax was born. It is to some a bleak,
grey city to-day—a city of cold, rain, mist, and
snow. It is the key city of the "Maritimes". To
many seamen from other lands it is Canada. When
Canada's greatest highway, the St. Lawrence River,
freezes over and the great port of Montreal is sealed
by ice, Halifax and its next-door-neighbour Saint
John, New Brunswick (the capital of Newfoundland is St. John's) deal with the country's exports
across the Atlantic. In war Halifax is as much a
fortress as Malta or Gibraltar. Many ships and con-
voys of friendly countries have sought shelter and
gathered their strength within the broad security of
Bedford Basin; to many of their crews the steep,
narrow streets of this two-hundred-year-old city
became for a time almost as familiar as the streets of
their home town. Halifax has long been a sailors'
town. In the marriage registry of St. Paul's Church,
Nelson's Captain Hardy and his bride set their
names which may be read there to-day. The few
survivors of the *Titanic* were taken to the city
and nearly two hundred of those who perished
are buried there. Halifax has known the dinners,
receptions, and all the sophistication of an important

MONTREAL AND THE ST. LAWRENCE

A NEW BRUNSWICK RIVER : LOGS ON
THEIR WAY TO THE MILL

HARVESTING IN ALBERTA

eighteenth-century garrison town; it has known sudden tragic disaster when, during the First World War, the French ammunition ship *Mont Blanc* blew up in the harbour with a gigantic explosion which devastated a large section of the city as effectively as German bombs flattened parts of English cities. Two thousand people were killed; six thousand were wounded; ten thousand were made homeless. Then, as the tidal wave of this explosion receded, the shipping in the harbour was sucked under the surging waters. Halifax has known the prosperity of good trade and, more than any other part of Canada, the personal impact of war. Through it all Halifax has known the sea; it has understood the sea; it has been understood by the men of the sea.

III
FRENCH CANADA

CANADA is a country of two languages. On any tin of soup, box of soap-flakes, or dollar bill, English and French appear side by side. It is sometimes thought, by people of other lands, that when Canadians refer to their country as bi-lingual they mean that most Canadians speak two languages. Unfortunately this is not so. Many positions in government or trade require men who do speak both French and English, but the vast majority of English-speaking Canadians know only as much French as they have learned in school which, as readers will know, is seldom enough to converse fluently. There are also many thousands of French-speaking Canadians who cannot make themselves understood in English.

Differences of religion and culture, too, widen the gap between the French and English-speaking Canadians, and not until there is better understanding will a truly united Canada arise.

The early history of the Province of Quebec is, to a large extent, the early history of Canada. It is a story of explorer, trader, Indian, and white man; it is a tale of martyred missionaries and endurance in the forest wilderness; it is an account of the early attempts of Canadian agriculture and of Canadian politics; it is, in fact, the first chapter in the opening up and development of the interior of this huge country.

Of all the men who played a part in this making

of French Canada no group were more steadfast of purpose or courageous of effort than the Jesuit missionaries. Driven on by a burning desire to save the souls of the savages of the forest, the "mysterious strangers garbed in black" faced hardship, famine, torture, and death. When Father Brébeuf believed himself about to be killed by the Hurons with whom he had been working he wrote to his superior: "We are perhaps about to give our blood and our lives in the cause of our Master, Jesus Christ. It seems that His goodness will accept this sacrifice, as regards me, in expiation of my great and numberless sins, and that He will thus crown the past services and ardent desires of all our Fathers here."

Brébeuf and his companions saved their lives on this occasion by giving a farewell feast for their captors at which they so impressed the Indians with their unflinching calm in the face of death that they won themselves a reprieve. Twelve years later Brébeuf's services were rewarded by the death he had faced so often. With a fellow priest, Lalemant, he was working with the Hurons of St. Louis when word came of an Iroquois band moving in to attack. Brébeuf's converts urged him to escape, but running for his life was not in the nature of Brébeuf. His companion, although physically weak, was a bold spirit. The early forest dawn was shattered suddenly when a tiger-like rush of screeching Iroquois swept out of the dark woods. Twice the hard-pressed Huron defenders fought back the assault and twice the swarms of Iroquois came swooping back. In a short time the fort and Indian dwellings were ablaze. Brébeuf and his friend Lalemant were taken. Stripped and bound they were led back to St. Ignace "where all turned out to wreak their fury on the two priests, beating them savagely with sticks and clubs as they drove them into the town". The next day the wild triumph of a few hours earlier gave way to an equally hysterical panic. Believing themselves about to be attacked by a huge army of Hurons the Iroquois prepared for flight. For a moment the hearts of the captives beat high with hope but the Iroquois were as cruel in defeat as in victory. When Huron and Jesuit did arrive at St. Ignace it was to find the settlement burned to the ground. Among the ashes of the town were the charred bodies of Brébeuf and Lalemant still tied to the stakes as they had been left.

In this brave story of New France, the name of one man is prominent. Samuel de Champlain who was born in a little village on the Bay of Biscay and died at the age of sixty-eight in Fort St. Louis, Quebec, deserves more than any other man the proud title "Founder of New France". Cartier, of whom we spoke in the previous chapter, may be said to have found New France but Champlain, with an interest, energy, and wisdom which extended far beyond mere exploration, was really the "founder". He has been called "the greatest figure of all Canadian history". Champlain's story is one of faith— faith in this wild forest-covered land of rock, great lakes, and rushing rivers.

To understand this story one must imagine a huge, unknown tract of country through which flows the St. Lawrence—a river so broad that its early explorers believed it to be the long-dreamed-of north-west passage to India and the Far East; a river so huge that its gulf is like the open sea. One must imagine this land inhabited only by half-naked, warring tribes of barbaric natives, and fur-bearing animals of many sorts whose skins were to be the gold of the New World. Up this river came the men of France—Cartier, who in his little ship *Emerillon* with its high stem and square sails, pushed up the St. Lawrence as far as what is now Montreal and found himself warmly welcomed by a host of Indians from the village of Hochelaga, Marquette, Joliet, Radisson, Groseilliers, La Salle, La Verendyre, and many others. The fingers of their exploration reached south to the Gulf of Mexico, west to within sight of the great western mountains we now call the Rockies and north into territory which is still much as it was in their day. The hand of France lay ever more firmly over a large part of the continent. Other nations, however, Britain in particular, were not prepared to stand by and watch that hand slowly tighten its grip on this new and richly fertile country. Forces were at work to pry those fingers loose.

The story of the bitter struggle between French and English is long and complicated. It involves the history of Indian wars and massacres in which savage tribes—Iriquois, Huron, Algonquin—led and misled by the white men who had come to take their nation, battled each other to the death for the gain of their European conquerors; it involves the history of the beaver, the demand for whose fur to make beaver hats for the fashionable in France and England, was at the root of the rivalry of the two countries; it involves the heroic attempts of men of God, in particular the Jesuits, to convert the heathen native to Christianity, in the face very often of bitter and often fatal hostility from heathen and fur trader alike. It involves the history of pioneer settlers, refugees from Europe, who came to build for themselves a new life in a new land and who found too often that Indian, fur trader and the inhospitality of wilderness and weather kept the question of existence itself constantly before their eyes.

The last chapter of the story is written in many hands but mainly in the hand of General Wolfe. It was in 1759, less than two centuries ago, that Wolfe launched the final and decisive campaign against New France—against the "American Gibraltar"—Quebec. With his army Wolfe clambered up the cliffs to face Montcalm and his army at dawn on the heights above, the famous Plains of Abraham. Montcalm, with few men at his command, made the only decision possible in the circumstances—attack at once. "The enemy is entrenching," he said, "and already has two cannon. If we give him time to make his position good we can never attack him with the troops we have." The French army advancing "with flags flying and uttering their war cry in the old time fashion", advanced in irregular, broken, and hastily formed columns against "the red uniforms of the English and the Highlanders' tartans". They fought with desperate courage but against the well directed fire of the larger British army they stood little chance of doing more than perishing bravely. The British general died in the hour of victory. Wounded three times, Wolfe staggered and, seeing that he was losing consciousness, he said to an officer of artillery who was near him: "Support me; my brave soldiers must not see me fall". Lieutenant Brown, of the grenadiers, Grenadier Henderson, and another soldier, ran forward and bore him to the rear, where, at his request, they laid him on the grass in a hollow of the ground. One of the officers volunteered to go in search of a surgeon. "It is useless," sighed the general, "I'm done for."

He was apparently unconscious when one of those supporting him cried: "They run! They run!"

"Who run?" Wolfe quickly asked, as if just awakened from a deep sleep.

"The enemy," replied the officer, "they give way everywhere."

Wolfe replied: "One of you run quickly to Colonel Burton and tell him to descend in all haste with his regiment towards the St. Charles River, seize the bridge and cut off the retreat." He then turned on his side, murmuring, "God be praised, I die happy," and expired.

The French General died in the hour of bitter defeat.

The artillery officer who acted as his secretary during the siege was near him trying to save one of the cannon. He says, "I saw M. Montcalm arrive on horseback supported by three soldiers. I entered the city with him, where the Chevalier de Bernetz gave me some orders which I ran to carry out on the ramparts. The crowd which had rushed out to see the issue of the combat, was returning and crowded the St. Louis Gate when some women seeing him pass, pale and covered with blood, cried out, 'O, My God! My God! the marquis is killed!'

"A surgeon, Arnoux, who came to see him, examined his wounds.

"'Is the wound a mortal one?' asked Montcalm.

"'Yes,' replied Arnoux, concealing nothing.

"'I am content,' replied Montcalm, 'how much longer have I to live?'

"'Not twenty-four hours,' was the reply.

"'So much the better,' returned the dying man. 'I shall not live to see the English masters of Quebec.'"

New France had passed and French Canada had been born. The culture of French Canadians to-day; their way of life; their loves and loyalties are no longer those of France any more than of Britain. The idea that they are the first true Canadians is deeply implanted in their minds. Montcalm's dying words still find a place in their hearts.

Montreal, Canada's biggest city, in spite of being a thousand miles from the sea, is one of the world's busiest seaports. The vast St. Lawrence Seaway which has recently been completed will make it even more so. It is the only city in Canada one might compare to a cosmopolitan European capital. Montreal has for Canadians something of the reputation that Paris has for Englishmen. It is a city of exciting restaurants and of great churches. It is a blend of the European and the North American. It is the archway to Canada. It is not, on the whole, a quaint and picturesque place. It is a modern, rushing, bustling city—of big business, big houses, and dreary slums. Its most beautiful part is on the leafy hill where McGill University stands and from which Jacques Cartier once surveyed the surrounding country. The casual visitor might at first be inclined to think the city much more English than it actually is. The fashionable hotels and shopping districts, the railway stations—although their employees may speak English with an accent and the English signs are duplicated in French—might well mislead the visitor into underestimating the strength of the French element. The French-Canadians and British-Canadians do not, as a rule, live in the same districts. The French, however, outnumber the British by nearly three to one. In Quebec City, with its great fortress-like hotel dominating the town, the population is almost entirely French-speaking. In the smaller towns and villages and across the farmsteads of the province French is an essential to understanding. The province is governed by French civil law.

Quebec is the largest of Canadian provinces. It is second largest in population and in industrial importance. Its area is six times that of Great Britain. Yet here, more than anywhere else in Canada, one may find the simple rural life of farm and village going on from generation to generation almost unchanging and with the parish priest the most respected and influential man in the community.

IV

ONTARIO

ONTARIO is an inland province with a salt water coastline of 600 miles along Hudson Bay, and a fresh water coastline along the Great Lakes and their connecting rivers of over 1,600 miles. Ontario is a province of lush, green orchards and rolling parkland; of hard, rocky regions where pine trees clinging to the stone, somehow find sustenance in the half-inch covering of soil. It is a land of bitter cold in the north, and of wine grapes and tobacco in the heat of the south; of agriculture and industry; of city and wilderness. Ontario is a big province —the second biggest in Canada. To Western Canadians, Ontario represents "the East"—a land of big cities and wealth. In contrast to Quebec, French Canada, the Province of Ontario is very definitely British Canada.

After the American Revolution large numbers of men and women who preferred life under British rule streamed north into Canada. Some settled in Nova Scotia; others in Quebec, and many, in response to the invitation of Governor Simcoe (who was Governor of Upper Canada, as Ontario was then called) came to settle in this region, particularly in the fertile Niagara Peninsula. As Lower Canada, or Quebec, strove aggressively to maintain and develop its peculiarly French tradition, so Upper Canada, or Ontario, strove to maintain and strengthen its peculiarly British way of living.

To people in the newer parts of Canada, where communities have grown from settlements to cities within living memory, Ontario appears as an old and historic province. Toronto, a great rushing city of tall buildings and a million people, gives no evidence of ever having known pioneer days. Yet, two hundred years ago, it was a poorly constructed fur trade fort in the middle of the forest—a fort which was too small, its occupants considered, ever to withstand an attack by hostile Indians. It was called Fort Toronto. In tracing briefly its growth from frontier fort to industrial city, we are tracing the growth of a host of other Canadian towns from small gatherings of men in the wilderness to sizeable towns or cities.

There is no general agreement among experts on which Indian language supplied the name Toronto, nor on its meaning which may be "place of meeting" or "an opening into a lake". The Fort, which never did a very roaring business, was in use for only nine years but as late as 1813 its ruins remained and are referred to by the American commander who captured York as "the ruins of the ancient French fort of Tarento". Towards the end of the eighteenth century Governor Simcoe and his wife arrived in Upper Canada. Mrs. Simcoe, fascinated by this new wild world about her, has left us in her diary an account of some of her early impressions and experiences. On 13th May 1793, she tells us of her husband's visit to Toronto. "Colonel Simcoe returned from Toronto, and speaks in praise of the harbour, and a fine spot near it covered with large oaks, which he intends to fix as a site for a town." Even as the town gradually came into being and official blue-prints were drawn up, the plans were still very little more than symbolic. One of the main streets for example, Ontario Street, was hardly more than a widening of the portage track over which men carried canoes and supplies between the lake and the bay.

The Simcoes departed. A new governor called for a meeting of the legislature to be held in Toronto. Writing to a local official he said: "You will therefore be pleased to apprise the inhabitants of the town that twenty-five gentlemen will want board and lodging during the session, which may possibly induce them to fit up their houses and lay in provisions to accommodate them." Toronto was still small enough to be excited over the arrival of twenty-five people. A traveller a year later described it as ". . . a dreary dismal place, not even possessing the characteristics of a village. There is no church, schoolhouse, nor in fact any of the ordinary signs of civilisation. There is no inn; and those travellers who have no friends to go to, pitch a tent and live there while they remain."

The town continued to grow. New buildings sprung up. An advertisement in the Upper Canada *Gazette* read as follows: "Toronto Coffee House—William Cooper begs leave to acquaint his friends and the public that he has erected a large and convenient stable on his own lot opposite the Toronto Coffee House, and stored it well with hay and oats of the very best quality. Travellers will meet with genteel and comfortable accommodation at the above house and their horses will be carefully attended to." There was now an inn!

THE PARLIAMENT BUILDINGS AT OTTAWA, WITH THE
INTER-PROVINCIAL BRIDGE TO HULL, QUEBEC

NIAGARA FALLS, ONTARIO

Friendless travellers no longer needed to bring their own tents. The Toronto Coffee House is no more. Not far from where it once stood, the mighty $18,000,000 Royal York Hotel, largest hotel in the British Empire, now towers up.

The early Torontonians, in common with all early settlers, were their own architects, contractors, and builders. Their cabins were of logs or thick boards laboriously shaped by heavy double-headed axes. Their rough-hewn furniture, some of which is still in existence, consisted of bare essentials—tables, chairs, and beds. The large front door opened into a living-room. On one side was the fireplace which commonly gave light, heat, and means of cooking. On the other side was a bedroom where the beds were often like wide shelves against the wall. A garret with little windows was more often than not the children's sleeping quarters. The community spirit was precious and strong in a country where each man was dependent on his neighbours for companionship and protection from the hazards of this pioneer frontier life. "Bees" were organised at which men, women, and children from the surrounding district banded together to build a house, erect a barn, plough fields, clear land, build fences, butcher and dress pigs, and so on. These "bees" served a twofold purpose of getting a sizeable job done quickly for an individual, or the community at large, and also as a pleasant social occasion for families in a land where people were entirely dependent on self-made entertainments to lighten their hard days.

So Toronto slowly emerged out of the forest. It grew and prospered, and is still growing. On the outskirts of the city, new streets are being laid out and new houses, thousands of them, are being built. An Indian on the streets now is a curiosity.

The city of Ottawa, capital of Canada, is also in Ontario. It is, like most Canadian and British cities, badly planned. Except for the Parliament Buildings, which strongly resemble their British counterparts and are very handsome indeed, the city is homely, in places even ugly. The site on the banks of the Ottawa River has been largely spoiled by factory chimneys and power houses. But the importance of Ottawa depends neither on its site nor its beauty. It is the capital of Canada and is fast becoming a world capital. The planning which takes place in Ottawa may do little to improve the appearance of the city, but it can do much to improve the appearance of the world, and of that planning we shall have more to say later.

The place names of a province tell us a good deal about its early inhabitants. The homesick Englishmen and Scots who settled in Upper Canada recalled the places they had left behind. Hamilton, London, Chatham, Stratford, Watford, and Craigleith are all Ontario cities and towns whose christeners looked back to their youth and the "folks at home". It would be wrong, however, to suppose that the influence of Canada's second race is not felt here. Sault Ste. Marie, Pointe Au Baril, Deux Rivières, and Bellevue are some of the many French names. And across Ontario, as across the whole of Canada, there are thousands of names given by Canada's first citizens— the Indians—Timiskaming, Attawapiskat, Wawa, Kapuskasing, and Ombabika.

TORONTO WITH THE ROYAL YORK HOTEL IN BACKGROUND (RIGHT)

A MOUNTIE, NEAR BANFF, ALBERTA

VANCOUVER, BRITISH COLUMBIA

V

THE WEST

THE great stretch of prairie, mountain, and forest which extends from Ontario to the Pacific is known as "The West". This huge area, containing the four provinces—Manitoba, Saskatchewan, Alberta, and British Columbia is the land of wheat, of oil, the pulp forests, the "sockeye" salmon, and the land of the Rocky Mountains. It is a land of many races, British, French, German, Japanese, Ukrainian, Icelandic, Asiatic Indian, and a hundred others. It is a land too of many faiths. In Edmonton, the capital of Alberta, there are not only a large number of churches for the various religions embraced by western protestants, catholics, and Jews, but there are several Russian Greek Orthodox churches and a Mohammedan Mosque with its domes and minaret. The West is new and raw and warm-hearted. It was explored late and was late in its admission to the Confederation. Alberta and Saskatchewan have been provinces on an equal basis with the older members of the Dominion for just over fifty years.

The older and more thickly populated eastern parts of Canada know three things about the "Prairie Provinces"—Manitoba, Saskatchewan, and Alberta. They grow wheat; they produce oil; they are cold in winter. All three things are true. Canada is the fourth greatest wheat producing country in the world and the great bulk of this wheat comes from the rolling plains of these three

sister provinces. Canada produces more oil than
any other country in the Commonwealth and again
the bulk of it comes from the West. Lastly, Canada
does produce some cold weather and some of the
coldest is found in these provinces. The temperature
in winter can go down to fifty degrees below zero
(i.e. some eighty degrees of frost). In the regions
of Southern Alberta which can be reached occasionally during the winter by warm winds from the
Pacific which find their way through the Rockies,
the temperature may rise sixty or more degrees in
two or three hours. In Calgary, Alberta, it may
be a bitter cold snowy morning calling for heavy
coats, scarves, and mitts and an evening so mild
that even a light coat is unnecessary. These warm
Pacific winds are called Chinooks.

The three Prairie Provinces are all about the
same size, each about twice the area of the British
Isles. At the time of Canadian Confederation in
1867 the population of all this vast region west of
the Great Lakes was less than 100,000. This
wilderness, dotted here and there with Hudson's
Bay Company fur trading posts, was "a sea of
prairie grass where the American buffalo still
roamed in great herds. British Columbia was in
its infancy and was an almost unknown Pacific
province isolated from the rest of Canada by
hundreds of miles of unoccupied land." To induce
people to move west and open up this huge plain
the Canadian government offered land for sale
at about two shillings an acre.

The settlement of "The West" has not always
been peaceful and has never been easy. Men who
were brave enough or foolhardy enough to leave

the more civilised East on a hope and a gamble that they might find a living beyond the western frontier, were seldom men who took kindly to rules and regulations sent out by the government civil servants of Upper Canada. The West was their land; they would make their own rules and live their lives in their own way. The present arrangement in Canada of provinces with certain rights and powers of their own bound together under a central government has evolved fairly quickly as government evolution goes, but it has not evolved painlessly. Just as the American colonies fought England for the right to govern themselves, so various groups in Canada, distrustful of a central government, lashed out angrily at the men who were attempting to unify this huge country under one law. Of all the western pioneers who shared in the bitterness of this struggle for a self-government, the name of Louis Riel is predominant.

"The dark threads of classic tragedy form the fabric of the Riel story. This strange intense man with the brooding spirit went to his death on the scaffold after a swift fifteen-year span of events which changed the history of Canada. In that time—a decade of it spent in exile—Riel's name fired the north west like a prairie blaze. He sparked two rebellions, marked by massacre, prayer, cannon war, and execution, twice set up provisional government with himself as president, ran successfully for federal parliament while a hunted fugitive with a price on his head, went insane, recovered, taught school, wrote poetry and, in effect, fathered the new province of Manitoba."

Riel was hanged in 1885. When asked on the

scaffold if he had anythiug to leave to his people he replied: "Only my heart and I gave that to my people fifteen years ago." To-day some people think of Riel as a fanatic and others as a great man. The spirit of Riel was in large measure the fighting spirit of Western Canada—a rough and tough spirit in a rough and tough lann. The West, in spite of the evidence of Holywood movies, is not nearly as rough and tough as it used to be. Manitoba, Saskatchewan, and Alberta are peaceful and productive provinces. But Riel is not entirely dead. The people of the West still pride themselves on their pioneer background and on a certain independence of spirit. The West is still new enough to be excited at the rapidity of its progress and the dreams of its future. It has known the wild excitement and panic of "boom" towns and gold strikes, and it has known the misery of crop failures, drought, and semi-starvation. Post-war oil development, particularly in Alberta, has resulted in a sudden influx of money and people, but the West is still essentially agricultural. It has grown the best grains in the world and has seen some of the world's worst farmers (a newly arrived Englishman once sowed his fields with rolled oats and wondered that he had no crop).

Winnipeg is the largest of the prairie province cities. It is the capital of Manitoba, a city of wide streets and bitter winter winds. It has a fine Parliament Building with a "golden boy" on the top of the dome. It is the headquarters of Western agriculture. Like Regina, the capital of Saskatchewan and Edmonton, the capital of Alberta, Winnipeg is a city of wooden frame houses and brightly coloured roofs. In all these Western cities the visiting European would be struck first by the temporary look of the houses. There are indeed stone and brick houses and some fine solid looking buildings, but the great bulk of the construction has been of wood. Yet there is something bright and fresh looking about many such houses however small and impermanent they might look beside their grey stone European sisters. And there is, too, a pride of community in the Western towns. Many of them, placed like match-boxes on a billiard table, began their careers with few natural advantages, but trees have been planted, small parks have been laid out, gardens have been trimmed, and bright paints have been applied lavishly. Of some of their other enterprises we shall have more to say later.

British Columbia is walled off from the rest of the country by the Rocky Mountains. It is a province of high wooded hills and mountains; of irrigated orchards and dense forests. Along its shore, which is indented and steep like the coast of Norway, are fishing villages and pulp mills. On Vancouver Island, lying off the coast, the capital of the Province, Victoria, is situated. It is commonly believed, and with a certain amount of truth, that the islanders consider themselves more English than the English and that there are more retired Colonels per square mile living here than anywhere else in the world. But Victoria does not mind being laughed at. Each year thousands of Canadians and Americans "follow the birds to Victoria" for a holiday and in later life, when working days are over, many return to enjoy the mild "English" climate in this city on the Pacific. Vancouver, the biggest city in the West, has a huge natural harbour. Vancouver is a wide, sprawling city. It has a beautiful and famous park called Stanley Park; it has a magnificent bridge called the Lyons Gate; it has some fine buildings and a number of beautiful homes. It is not, however, a beautiful city. Its beauty lies in its surroundings rather than itself—the orchard and mountain country behind it; the wooded fiords and bays to the North and South, the blue Pacific, and the Straits of Juan de Fuca which lie before it. To Vancouver have come in the past many men from the East—Japanese and Indians. It is a big and growing city, a busy and ever busier port. It is Canada's Western outpost looking out across the Western ocean to the ancient lands of the far East.

of their sleep, and had neither time nor power to make any resistance; men, women, and children, in all upwards of twenty, ran out of their tents stark naked, and endeavoured to make their escape; but the Indians having possession of all the land-side, no place could they fly for shelter. One alternative only remained, that of jumping into the river, but, as none of them attempted it, they all fell a sacrifice to Indian barbarity. The shrieks and groans of the poor expiring wretches were truly dreadful."

A few years after Hearne's journey Alexander Mackenzie, an employee of the rival North West Company, voyaged down the huge river which bears his name from Great Slave Lake to the Arctic Ocean. It was a long and perilous voyage in birch-bark canoes. Towards the end, as they paddled on through the long hours of never ending daylight they began to lose heart. "The prospect about the travellers was gloomy and dispiriting. The low banks of the river were now almost treeless, except that here and there grew stunted willow, not more than three feet in height. The weather was cloudy and raw, with gusts of rain at intervals . . . discontent grew apace: the guide was evidently at the end of his knowledge; while the violent rain, the biting cold, and the fear of an attack by hostile savages kept the voyagers in a continual state of apprehension." At last Mackenzie reached the delta of the river. When a great rushing tide at night threatened to swamp their baggage and drown their tents they knew they had reached the bleak shores of the northern sea.

Sir John Franklin, in command of two ships,

the *Erebus* and the *Terror*, vanished into this same northern sea forever. Valiant search expeditions which followed pieced together a tale of stark tragedy. From the lips of Eskimos they heard of the abandonment of the crushed and frozen ships and of a march across the ice towards Back's Fish River—a march which was never finished. The skeleton of one of Franklin's men, sprawled in the snow with the head towards the river, completed the story.

Exploration went on. Markham, Lockwood, Peary, and Nansen all in succession pushed farther and farther north. A teacher in a technical school in Stockholm, Professor Andree, together with two friends attempted to cross over the Pole in a specially constructed balloon. A brisk south wind carried them north from Spitzbergen where the balloon was launched and a carrier pigeon message two days later spoke of them moving steadily towards their goal. The rest was silence: the bodies of Andree and his companions were found in 1930, together with his diaries, which have been published. The final prize fell to Captain Peary of the U.S. Navy. He was the first white man to reach the Pole. Within a radius of some miles he saw nothing but snow. There was no sign of land. The top of the world was cold and silent.

What of the northland to-day? It is still an unexplored and forbidding wilderness, known to very few and by those few known only in part. The natives of the north are the Eskimos—a short, strong, swarthy people whose racial origin is still to some extent a matter of doubt. Deep in the silence of this frozen land the Eskimo lives a happy life according to his own rules. The range of this thinly scattered people extends right across the top of North America and an almost unlimited distance northward, but the bands are small and the numbers few. The Eskimo is a peace-loving, contented person whose life consists almost entirely in working to survive—hunting and fishing. Along the Arctic coast where caribou are scarce, the seal is the staff of life. It provides clothing, meat, and oil for heating and cooking. In the season of open water the hunter in his small kayak may hunt walruses with a harpoon, a dangerous sport.

To a large extent the Eskimo's life has been unchanged by the white man. He lives as he has always done in a skin tent by summer and an igloo by winter; his main diet consists largely of raw flesh: reindeer, seal, white whale, walrus and on occasion polar bear and Arctic hare. His family connections remain vague and irresponsible by our standards, but as more and more interest is taken in the North, so the white man comes more and more in touch with the men of the North. The Eskimo uses new weapons and implements; the sick native brought south for medical treatment returns to his people with strange tales of the things he has done and the marvels he has seen; missionaries teach the Eskimos new faiths and their children are collected to learn of books and numbers, and of the unhappy world of war and fear. All this is bound to come, but whether the simple native of the northern wilderness can survive the new civilisation which slowly, but certainly, is grasping him, no man can say for sure.

VII

TRANSPORTATION

THE area of Canada is only slightly less than the area of the whole continent of Europe. In all this land there were, a little over a hundred years ago, fewer than 70 miles of railroad. To-day there are over 40,000 miles. To anyone who has paused to think of the vast extent of this country and the tremendous distances which separate city from city the difficulty of binding Canadians together as a unified people must be obvious. Many different influences have been at work in the uniting and fusing together of the Canadian people but no single factor has been as important as that of communication: roads, railways, aeroplanes, postal services, telegraphic facilities, telephones, and all those means by which one Canadian, perhaps several thousand miles away, is able to talk with or visit another Canadian comfortably and quickly. There are two main railway companies in Canada: the Canadian National Railway, owned by the Government, and the Canadian Pacific Railway which is a private company. Each of these has a sister airline company: Trans-Canada Air Lines, Government owned, and Canadian Pacific Air Lines, privately owned.

The first railway line in Canada was a short stretch of a few miles which followed an old portage trail near the St. Lawrence. A locomotive, imported from England, was manipulated on to the track but could not be induced to move. It steamed gently, but was as stationary as a kettle. "Experts" were sent for from the United States. They checked the engine over and found it to be in excellent condition. They only discovered what the trouble was when the Canadian operators attempted once again to make the thing "go". Fearful of an explosion, its owners had not put enough water in the boiler or a hot enough fire in the fire-box.

The real beginnings of trans-Canada railroading are confused by government scandal and shady financing. British Columbia, isolated in the West, became restless at the delay and uncertainty of government policy in the East. It had entered Confederation on the promise of a railroad which would link it with the rest of Canada. Now it considered breaking away from the country to which it was so loosely tied. At length, however, in 1881, the Canadian Pacific Railway Company was formed with money, land grants, and a few incomplete sections of track totalling some 700 miles. Five years later engineers and construction men had spanned the country with a steel road and had built what was then the longest railway line in the world. The difficulties and dangers encountered by its builders make a story of romance and adventure which will be told as long as this country survives. The work of construction through miles of dense forest, through the Rockies, across turbulent mountain streams and dangerous gullies where landslides in summer and avalanches of snow and ice in winter threatened to obliterate both men and railway, has never been surpassed. The work was advanced with remarkable speed. In one year the builders averaged two and a half miles of track a day. Five years before the contracted time the railway was completed. On 28th June 1886 the first trans-continental train left Montreal for Port Moody, the forerunner of Vancouver.

In one sense the difficulties had just begun. Now that the railway was finished there was very little to carry on it. Bleached buffalo bones for fertilizer were among the first shipments east. The expansion of the West, as we have seen, has been recent and rapid. Now that the West was "opened up" European immigrants were encouraged by both the railway and the government to settle there. A giant milling operation, the greatest in the world, was installed at Lake-of-the-Woods. Wheat began to pour east; farm machinery and would-be farmers headed west. A silk trade was established with Japan through Vancouver, and special silk trains roared across the country bringing the raw silk east for processing. The West had become an integral part of Canada.

Other railway lines were in existence. Thirty years before the C.P.R., the Grand Trunk line was carrying passengers and freight from Montreal to Toronto, doing particularly good business when the Great Lakes and St. Lawrence were frozen. The Champlain and St. Lawrence Railroad, operating a line of sixteen miles during the summer only, used horse-drawn carriages some fifty years before the C.P.R. By 1915 the Grand Trunk Pacific had extended its line also to the west coast, and a company called the Canadian Northern was hopefully planning yet a third trans-continental railway. The 1914–18 war hit the railways hard. In the autumn of 1917 the Canadian Government decided to take these railways over. The Canadian Northern, the Grand Trunk, the Grand Trunk Pacific, the Intercolonial, and the National Transcontinental were consolidated and the present Canadian National Railway Company was born.

Canadian trains are bigger and more powerful than those of Britain. They are designed to haul passengers and freight over much greater distances and consequently must be designed to be "lived in" to a greater extent than British trains, and to carry a greater volume of freight at one time. "Sleepers" or "berths", as they are called in these trains, are more private and more like beds. There are also smoking cars and lounges for the comfort of passengers who are probably going to be on the train for a few days, rather than a few hours.

Canadian railways, of course, face special problems which hardly concern the railways of Britain. The maintaining of service over some 40,000 miles of track through the long and severe winters of this immense country, calls for careful planning and special equipment. All preparations for winter operations are completed by 15th September of each year and everything must be kept in readiness for snowstorms and severe low temperatures until 1st. May Over the years the railways have developed a remarkable system for keeping their lines clear of snow. There are snow ploughs which can buck drifts up to a height of fifteen feet; there are snow blowers which suck up the snow and blow it clear; there are trucks with revolving brooms, bulldozers ice cutters, snow removal trucks, and melting pits. There is also a "snow melter" which consists of a snow loader and a large tank mounted on a car which melts the snow and ejects it later as water. Each year the railways employ some thousands of extra men to assist in keeping lines clear of snow. In addition, turn-tables must be heated to prevent freezing and underground cables have been installed in places where icing is liable to break overhead lines. Figures are often dull and always difficult to remember, but it may serve to show the extent of this problem of winter operation of railways if we know that the C.P.R. alone has spent over one million pounds in a winter for snow removal, and that snow ploughs on the Eastern lines have travelled 89,089 miles in a single month. Occasionally, in spite of all efforts, passenger trains have been trapped for days by tracks blocked with snow.

The two main airlines of Canada have, in their years of operation, extended their range far beyond the shores of this country. They provide now a swift and safe service, not only between all the main cities of Canada, but virtually around the world. There is no country in the world to which travel by air has meant more than to Canada. An Edmonton lawyer having business in Toronto can leave his office at noon, reach Toronto that evening, conduct his business the following morning, have lunch and arrive home that night, if he travels by air. He has been away from home for a day and a half. By train it will take him three nights and two days to get there and the same to return. Even if he only spends a day in Toronto he will be away from home for a week. There are,

CANADIAN PACIFIC DIESEL PASSENGER
TRAIN IN THE ROCKIES

TWO INDIAN BOYS WITH GOOD CAUSE TO SMILE

GRAIN ELEVATORS AT PORT ARTHUR

of course, many small settlements and isolated communities, particularly in the north country, which are not served by railway. For people in these outlying districts the aeroplane has frequently meant the difference between life and death. Before there was ever a regular trans-Canada air service brave and skilled men, flying small and often ill-equipped aircraft, made many perilous flights into unmapped and distant areas to bring medical aid to the sick or to carry back the sick or wounded to civilisation and hospital. The work of these "bush pilots" goes on to-day and the stories of their hardihood and daring are many. One pilot broke a propellor blade while making a forced landing on a frozen lake; hacking the opposite blade into the same shape he took off safely and completed his flight. Many others have faced storm and blizzard to bring help to those who live beyond the reach of road or railway.

In addition to rail and air services Canada has water and road transport. British readers will know as much about Canadian Pacific Steamships, which is a British owned company, as Canadians themselves. The Great Lakes, too, have their passenger and freight vessels, particularly grain boats and tankers. The twin-cities of Fort William and Port Arthur at "the head of the lakes" are the grain ports of Canada. From the vast storage elevators along the docks, grain is sucked into the holds of countless ships. The Great Lakes-St. Lawrence System, as this water route is called, is a vital artery in the economic life of Canada. With the completion of the Welland Ship Canal in 1930, the largest lake freighters can now come down river as far

D

as Kingston. If the United States will agree to Canada's dreamed-of plan for the St. Lawrence Seaway, these inland freighters will be able to meet their ocean-going sisters at Montreal.

In a country like Canada the great distances and small population make the construction and maintenance of cross-country roads an expensive and difficult undertaking. It is possible to drive across Canada, and a new trans-Canada highway is in process of construction, but most Canadians who wish to cross the country by car prefer to go south into the United States and back into Canada when they are just south of their destination. In the various provinces there are highways as good as any in the world, built, many of them, at tremendous cost, through rocky, and difficult country. There is, of course, a network of secondary roads, gravel and dirt, which link the various small farming and other rural communities with each other and with the larger cities.

VIII
THE MOUNTED POLICE

JOHN SOUNDING SKY, a Cree Indian, had a son called Almighty Voice. Under arrest for a series of wild and irresponsible crimes, Voice escaped during the changing of his guard, swam the Saskatchewan River, which was full of floating chunks of ice, collected his squaw and rifle and headed for the forest. Sergeant Colebrook of the "Mounties" was shot and killed in attempting to arrest the Indian's flight and Almighty Voice vanished into the wilderness. It seemed a hopeless task to follow him and bring him to Justice. The woods were his home and, despite his reputation, his relatives would protect and shield him. For a long year and a half, taunted by the newspapers and tormented by the cheap jeers of an ill-informed public, the Mounted Police followed every lead and clue until late one May evening Voice was tracked down and chased into a large grove of poplars and willows. Just to show he was still unrepentant he shot, and hit twice, one of his pursuers. Two others were shot while attempting to dislodge the wild man from his refuge. A volunteer helper and another "Mountie" were hit and killed before Voice's exact hiding-place was discovered and the murderer himself finally destroyed. The hunt had been a long one. It had cost the lives of two members of the Force and a civilian, but the growing legend was once again proved true. "The Mounties get their man."

In the year when the North West Mounted Police, as they were first named, came into existence, the then tiny settlement of Winnipeg was the only centre of any importance in the whole of the wide western plains. This half of Canada was still Indian country—hunting ground and battle ground, but certainly not territory for peaceful settlement. The Blackfeet, Bloods, and Piegans would tolerate no permanent trading posts and dealt only with unscrupulous free traders who brought them "fire-water". The protests of missionaries and Hudson's Bay Company men went unheard and as more and more freebooters swarmed into the area, so drunken bloodshed, the curse of smallpox, and general demoralisation spread across the West.

The Mounted Police were originally formed to deal with this situation; to go into this wild country, stop the traffic in spirits with the Indians, win their confidence, and establish law, order, and conditions suitable for peaceful settlement. There were only 300 of them—nearly all easterners from the Atlantic side of the Great Lakes—who set out on foot, horse, and ox-cart from the little settlement of Dufferin on the Red River, westward into this little known land. Only a tiny handful of them had any real idea of the territory they were entering, of the job they were undertaking or of the savages they were about to encounter. The long, hard journey was a cruel initiation, but it revealed a firmness of character and directness of purpose in the troop, which was not only to stand it in good stead during the following months but was to become characteristic of the whole Force in time to come. Their immediate objective was "Fort Whoop-Up", built by Missouri whisky traders and a central point for freebooters and illegal trading with the Indians. After more than two months of gruelling travel which had left them not far from exhaustion, they camped eventually in the Sweet Grass Hills not far from the border. "Fort Whoop-Up" had not yet been located but the worst of the march had been completed and not one man had been lost.

What lay ahead of them they could not guess with any certainty. They were not only prepared to fight "the savages", as they called them, but also the lawless men from south of the border who had established for themselves a highly profitable trade in buffalo robes and wolf skins. Half the group presently pushed north and west from their camp and, guided by a willing and intelligent half-breed, they arrived eventually among the foot-hills of the Rocky Mountains. On their way they had found "Fort Whoop-Up". It was completely deserted. There had still been no battle.

In the meantime the remaining half of the band had broken up into its various troops to cover key points across the prairies. It now became a matter of dispersal in order to round up and bring to justice the freebooters, and this dispersal meant the establishment of forts and posts at several points. At these posts very small groups of men, often completely isolated, and at best with little in the way of equipment, supplies, and supporters, were called upon to maintain law and order over vast areas which, until now, had scarcely known even the meaning of such words. With almost unbelievable speed and efficiency the Mounted Police brought the situation under control. There were some flare-ups; there was some bloodshed; but the purposeful authority of the Crown had been established.

The Indians had given to the traders a fortune in furs but the bargain was a one-sided one. Strangely enough—or perhaps not so strangely—there was almost no opposition to the new Force from the Indians. The wiser of them had long since learned that they were not selling furs alone; they were selling their lives; they were selling their very existence. In the summer of 1875 there came rumours of a threatening uprising among the Indians and French half-breeds near the Hudson's Bay Company post of Fort Carlton on the Saskatchewan River. The arrival of fifty Mounted Policemen having effectively discouraged any plans of revolt, the party proceeded on west and south to Fort Macleod. Near this place a council was held with several hundred of the once feared and fearless Blackfeet. With dignity, and the assurance that only comes with a mixture of wisdom and authority, Chief Crowfoot, great Ogehma of the Blackfeet and head of the Confederacy told the leaders of the Police that his people were pleased to have them in "his" country. A short time later when the Sioux Indians south of the border revolted against "the white intruder" and carried the battle north into Canada, Chief Crowfoot, in spite of repeated and urgent invitations, refused to support them in their bid to cast out the white men from the West. After the meeting at Fort Macleod, the fine old warrior, who had received the grateful thanks of Queen Victoria for his loyalty in time of trouble, signed on behalf of his people a treaty with the Canadian Government.

So the settlers came; the buffalos disappeared; ploughs broke the grassy plains; and the railway's steel road stretched out across the West. The land was far from peaceful. The 4,000 railway builders were, many of them, rough and troublesome. Although the Blackfeet accepted the coming of the white men, the disappearance of the buffalo and the drastic changes in their way of life led, not unnaturally, to unrest among disgruntled half-breeds and eventually to the ill-starred North-West Rebellion under the leadership of Louis Riel. Through it all the Blackfeet, the first friends of the "Mounties", remained loyal and steadfast and the Force conducted itself with the strong assurance for which it was already famous.

Over the years the Force grew not only in reputation, but also in strength. In the year 1920 the jurisdiction of the Royal North West Mounted Police was extended to cover the whole country in the enforcement of Dominion laws. In the same year the name was changed to the Royal Canadian Mounted Police. Since that time, most provinces have invited the R.C.M.P. to enforce Provincial Law as well within the borders of the individual provinces.

The R.C.M.P. has grown up with the country it guards and polices. It has become a large, complex, and highly scientific organisation. Its members only wear scarlet coats now on cere-monial occasions and are much more likely to be mounted on a motor-cycle or in a car, than on a

horse. There are marine and aviation divisions.
The officers of the Force are commissioned by the
Crown and for many years have been selected
from serving non-commissioned officers. But in
this day of mechanisation, mobilisation, and the
scientific study of criminology the R.C.M.P. have
never—even in the eyes of their fellow Canadians
—become mere dull symbols of law and order.
Small Canadian boys still want to grow up to
be "Mounties" and some do. As their motto
"Maintiens Le Droit" indicates, they do stand
for law and order, but they stand for something
far more than that.

There are still, as we have seen, wide areas of
Canada with only a sprinkled handful of inhabitants. Beyond the northern frontier, men live
lonely and isolated lives. In these outlying districts, on the very fringe of civilisation, as well as
in the heart of the busy cities, the R.C.M.P. carry
on their work as they did in the early days of the
West. The R.C.M.P. bring to these Canadians the
security of justice and so the scarlet coat still stands
for the courage of the pioneer. The erect figure,
who looks so impressive opening the door of a
princess's car or talking to a tourist in the Rockies,
is Canada's showman but he is also Canada's
policeman.

IX

THE HUDSON'S BAY COMPANY

IN every town or city of any size from Winnipeg west to Vancouver there is a Hudson's Bay Company store. Depending on the size of the community, these stores vary in size from little shacks with a bell over the door that announces the arrival of each customer, to big many-storied buildings with escalators, hidden lighting, and any number of different departments. Behind these many stores their lies a history—a history which is so closely woven into the very fabric of the history of Canada itself, that at times the story of the Company and the story of Canada became one and the same. We have already seen to what a large extent the beginnings of Canada depended on the fur trade. It was to trade in furs that the H.B.C. was formed and it is the active continuance of the same trade to-day which links the past with the present. Over two hundred posts are maintained by the Company in the northland to carry on the work which made it famous.

In the year 1670—one of the important dates in the history of this country—King Charles II signed a charter which, in effect, gave to the newly formed Company a very large part of what is now North America. He was giving away far more territory than he dreamed of—". . . those seas, straits and bays, rivers, lakes, creeks, and sounds . . . within the straits commonly called Hudson's Straits together with all the lands, countries, and territories upon the coasts and confines of the seas, straits, bays, lakes, rivers, creeks and sounds aforesaid. . . ." It has been pointed out that: "On a modern map, the Company received those portions of the Provinces of Ontario and Quebec north of the Laurentian watershed and west of the Labrador boundary, the whole of Manitoba, most of Saskatchewan, the southern half of Alberta, and a large portion of the North West Territories; in all a great basin of one million, four hundred and eighty-six thousand square miles."

The charter was granted to Prince Rupert as first Governor of the "Gentlemen Adventurers of England trading into Hudson's Bay".

But the Company's chartered rights to the trade of these territories was by no means undisputed. The bold French Canadians regarded the banks of the St. Lawrence River as their ground. The success of the English to the north and south of the French alarmed them. The establishment of H.B.C. posts in these areas was not only cutting into their profitable trade but was threatening to encircle them and endanger their very survival. For more than ten years the ruthless war of the fur trade was bitterly fought. Men were burned to death in their forts; naval skirmishes took place on the icy waters of Hudson Bay; bribed Indians were stirred up at times to raid and kill. Along with these attempts to destroy each other, went other more positive attempts to discover and open up new and untapped areas. Many are the stories of hardship, endurance, and wild adventure that can be told of these days.

Two of the most famous of the H.B.C. adventurers

were Pierre Radisson and his brother-in-law Groseilliers (who was known as Gooseberry). Radisson, whose explorations into the untracked wilderness of the North did so much, not only for the sometimes ungrateful Company which he served, but for the development of the country itself, came to the little town of Three Rivers as a young boy. The Radisson family had not long arrived from France before young Pierre's adventures started. He was hunting one day near the settlement when a band of Mohawk Indians seized him and carried him off back to their encampment. Here he was tied to a stake for burning, but the Mohawks wished to have some fun first. They began by tearing some of his fingernails out and then allowed some of their own youngsters to use him as a target for their arrows. So bravely did the lad bear these brutal tortures that they decided to spare his life. He was adopted by a Mohawk woman and became a favourite of the tribe. With some Algonquin captives he eventually made his escape and had nearly reached home when the pursuing Mohawks overtook him. Three of their number were killed in the struggle to recapture him and Pierre was once more bound to a post for burning on his return. Once again however his fortitude saved him and he was returned to his adopted Indian family. A second attempt at escape, some time later, succeeded and he sought refuge in a Dutch post at what is now Albany. From there he was sent to Holland from where he eventually found his way back to Three Rivers.

In the years that followed, Radisson, who became

a citizen of England, made many voyages and journeys on behalf of the Company. He schemed and worked; he went over to the French and came back to the English on two occasions; he worked and fought with Indians, Frenchmen, and his rivals within the Company. When war came with France he found himself distrusted. His annuity was cut. Eventually, after a battle in the English courts, he was granted in his old age an annual pension of one hundred pounds. He died in poverty.

There were others besides Radisson. One of these, a youth of twenty named Henry Kelsey, was almost certainly the first white man to look upon the prairies of Saskatchewan. He wrote rhymed introductions to his journals which show him to have been a much better explorer than poet.

> Now Reader Read for I am well assur'd
> Thou dost not know the hardships I endur'd
> In sixteen hundred and ninety'th year
> I set forth as plainly may appear
> Through God's assistance for to understand
> The natives' language and to see their land
> And for my masters' interest I did soon
> Sett from ye house ye twealth of June
> Then up ye River I with heavy heart
> Did take my way and from all English part
> To live among ye Natives of this place
> If God permits me for one two years space
> The Inland Country of Good report hath been
> By Indians but by English yet not seen . . .

Through the work of men like Radisson and Kelsey and through the agressive determination of its English governors, the H.B.C. extended its chain of forts and tightened its grip on the northland.

The French rival, hampered by jealousy and mismanagement in France which resulted in inadequate support coming too late, was being gradually hemmed in. The extent of the French empire of trade and exploration in North America had extended once as far south as the Gulf of Mexico and as far west as the Rocky Mountains, but it balanced "like a gigantic inverted pyramid . . . on the apex of the St. Lawrence lowland." It was a vast and increasingly unstable holding. As the H.B.C. slowly closed its hand on the St. Lawrence and as the British determination to win Canada for its own became more fixed, so the position of the French trader became less and ever less secure. We have already seen something of the struggle for supremacy in this part of Canada and of the final fall of New France.

With the disappearance of the French as a rival the H.B.C. was almost immediately faced with another in the shape of a band of ambitious and unscrupulous traders who, dismissed at first as mere "pedlars", soon formed themselves into the powerful North West Company which ". . . conquered half a continent, and built up a commercial empire the like of which North America at least has never seen." The Nor' Westers were mainly Scottish Highlanders whose fathers had fled north from the American Revolution or had fought under Wolfe at the taking of Quebec. They were fighters and they cared little for the rules. The Royal Charter of the H.B.C. meant nothing to them. They fought against the Company's charter in the courts and they fought against the Company's men whenever their own interests were threatened.

Of the men who brought the Company success, one man stands out above all others—Alexander Mackenzie—explorer, geographer, and trader who, travelling by canoe, in three months mapped the longest river of the continent, a river which still bears his name. Under his guidance and led by the man himself, the North West Company reached out northward to the Arctic and west to the Pacific.

The rivalry between the two companies grew in bitterness as the North West Company grew in strength. As in all such struggles between rival European interests in North America, no matter who won the Indian lost. Both sides played for the support of the "redskin" and both sides bought him with muskets and rum, a combination which has never proved healthy. From a commercial battle it was but a short step to a battle of blood. But the North West Company was a house divided against itself and it lacked the strong and stable backing which the H.B.C. could depend on. In the end the two joined forces and the famous North West Company was absorbed by its still more famous rival.

The million and a half square miles which had been granted the Company under the original charter were signed over at a time when men could not possibly foresee what the future of Canadian settlement might be. No one knew the huge extent of the territories which had been made over to the "Gentlemen adventurers". It was obviously impossible that any private company could hold this land in the now fast-developing country. The modern history of the Company begins with its sale to the Canadian Government, for a sum of three hundred thousand pounds, the land which had been given it by King Charles. The Company retained and retains to-day, only a few thousand acres of its once mighty empire.

If anyone should think that the glories of the Hudson's Bay Company belong only to the past, he has but to pick up a copy of the Company magazine *The Beaver* to realise to what a large extent the pioneering spirit of northern trade and exploration still flourishes in the Company. H.B.C. "trainees" still serve their time in the isolated forts and posts of the North West Territories and on the fringes of the Arctic Ocean. The trade with Indians and Eskimos is a friendly well-ordered business now and furs are exchanged for groceries and clothes rather than muskets and rum. The beaver, which was once Canada's emblem, has been replaced by the maple leaf, but the Company remains and the boy who buys a new pair of skates at a modern air-conditioned store with concealed lighting, escalators, and the latest ideas in interior decoration, is still dealing with the "Gentlemen Adventurers of England trading into Hudson Bay."

X

THE INDIANS

THE mastodon, the red deer, and the reindeer migrated in the far off past from Asia. It is probable that as these animals, along with various other mammals, moved slowly through the centuries down into North America, they were followed in in their migration by the men who depended on them for food and clothing. The origins of the first natives of Canada are uncertain, but it seems probable that some 20,000 years ago these men began to arrive on this continent. The men from Europe arriving on these shores and believing they had reached Asia, called the red-skinned inhabitants "Indians" and the name has remained. There were, at that time, something over 200,000 Indians in the country. Since then the population has slowly declined though of late years it has begun to show a slight increase.

The Indians were a backward people. They knew only one metal—copper. They had not discovered the wheel. Dependent as they were for food on the wild life of the forest they were an unsettled roaming race of people who, in times of great hunger, were capable of resorting to cannibalism. Left to themselves and to the natural processes of development, the Indians would have taken some thousands of years to reach the same state of civilisation as their European discoverers. But the Indian was not left to himself. The white men traded with him; fought with and against

WATERFOWL LAKE, IN THE ROCKIES

him; gave him advanced weapons and implements; converted him to new faiths; treated him as a friend and as an enemy, as a mature adult and as a child and, in the end, made a treaty with him by which the Indian agreed to live on special reserves set aside for his use. He is looked after by a government department and almost forgotten by his fellow Canadians.

The early history of Canada, of exploration and fur trade, is the story too of the Indians. The Indians of Canada can be divided according to language and further sub-divided by tribes. Those of the Algonquin stock, covering an area from the Atlantic to the Rocky Mountains, are the most numerous and include many famous tribes—the Micmacs of the Maritimes, the Montagnais of Quebec, the Ojibwas and Crees of Ontario and the prairies, and the Blackfeet of Alberta. Around Georgian Bay in an area known later as "Huronia", lived the Huron tribe. Perhaps the most famous of all Indians, however, are those of the Iriquois tribes. They were once known and feared under the name of the "Five Nations". They called themselves "Ongwanonsionni" and comprised the Cayugas, Mohawks, Oneidas, Onondagas, and Senecas. Later with the inclusion of the Tuscaroras they became the "Six Nations".

The Iriquois league, obtaining fire-arms from early Dutch and English traders, was quick to extend its territory at the expense of weaker and more peaceful neighbouring tribes. Quick to discover how profitable a monopoly of the fur trade might be to them, the Iriquois, hungry for battle and well armed, struck fiercely and brutally at the

E

Hurons, exterminating many and scattering the remainder. A frightened witness of one of their raids wrote in his diary: "They approach with stealth on silent feet but when the fight begins they are like savage animals. They kill with screams of delight. When all are dead or have escaped into the forest they are gone like shadows."

The Eries, too, were vanquished and the Iriquois ruled supreme. The English and Dutch with whom they traded were quick to encourage them in their distrust of the French and to secure the huge bulk of fine pelts for themselves. The very existence of New France itself was threatened by this iron control of the fur country of the Upper St. Lawrence. The Iriquois stranglehold was tightening. In the year 1652 not a single beaver pelt reached Montreal. Any Indian venturing down the St. Lawrence or Ottawa faced almost certain death. But the blockade was broken. Radisson and Groseilliers, the two young Frenchmen whose story reads like the wildest adventure yarn, headed off into the wilderness where beyond the Sault many hundreds of Indians were gathered waiting an opportunity to resume their trade with the French. Two years later a brave flotilla of fifty canoes manned by a strange mixed band of natives and led by the two triumphant young Frenchmen swept down the Ottawa River to Quebec. The guns of the fort and of the ships in the harbour boomed forth. New France was saved.

This, of course, is but one incident in the long history of war and counter-war between Indian and Indian, and Indian and White, in the early days of exploration, trade, and settlement. France urged certain tribes on against the English just as the English did against the French. Indians could often be bought with rum or brandy and both were cheap. The fur trade was a ruthless business. In all this grim story of brutal Indian battle at best ignored, at worst encouraged by European settlers and traders, the Indian was the ultimate loser. Confused and uncivilised he was no match in the end for the white men whom he had never really understood.

As the French and English increased in numbers, as the fur trade decreased in importance and as the settlement of Canada moved west so the power of the Indians decreased. Willing or unwilling there was little left for them to do but make permanent peace with their white conquerors who had come to take over their land. The terms varied slightly in the various treaties made with the several tribes, but in essence they were the same. It was agreed that in exchange for the surrender of their rights in the land the Crown undertook to set aside reserves and provide certain other benefits in the way of small annual cash payments and, in some cases, distribution of goods. The usual annual grant is $5.00 per head for Indians and $25.00 for Chiefs. Many tribes also have special hunting and fishing rights. In some cases the government has also assumed responsibility for elementary education, agricultural and other training and advice, and medical care. These rights the Indians forfeit if they leave their reserve land.

An abbreviated version of a typical treaty reads as follows: "July 20, 1906—Chippewyan, Cree and others—Northern Saskatchewan Area ceded 85,800 square miles.

"GOVERNMENT OBLIGATIONS.—Reserves up to one square mile for each family of five—subject to Government's right to deal with settlers on reserve lands, right to sell or lease reserve lands with the consent of the Indians and to appropriate reserve lands for federal public purposes subject to compensation for improvements and lands; education; right to hunt, trap and fish.

"TREATY PRESENTS.—Indians $12.00, Chiefs $32.00, Headmen $22.00; medals and flags.

"ANNUITY.—Chiefs $25.00, Headmen $15.00, Indians $5.00; distribution of twine and ammunition annually; triennial suit of clothes to Chiefs and Headmen."

The vast majority of Canadian Indians nowadays maintain themselves out of sight and out of mind of the rest of the population. Some, being excellent craftsmen, have made a profitable business of selling their handicraft. Birch-bark baskets skilfully adorned with porcupine quills, beaded jackets and moccasins, distinctive woollen sweaters, all find a ready sale, particularly among tourists. But for the most part the contact between white Canadians and Indians is slight. No longer is the Indian the colourful native pictured for us by early explorers. His dress of hides and his painted nakedness has given way to denim trousers and ragged shirts. The Indian in public is usually treated as something between a child and a curiosity. At rodeos and local fairs Chiefs, in the faded glory of feathered headdress and buckskin jacket, may sometimes be seen earning a few cents by allowing themselves to be photographed with children or a laughing party of tourists. At Banff in the Rockies an effort

XI

EDUCATION

A FEW years ago a Canadian schoolmaster visiting England was invited to lunch at one of the better-known English Public schools. He sat at a table with some of the older boys and attempted with almost no success to strike up a conversation with a very shy lad sitting next to him. Every question he asked was answered either by a shy silence or an embarrassed "yes" or "no". At length the poor schoolboy, obviously feeling that he was proving a very inadequate lunch companion to the visitor, turned suddenly and blurted out the startled and startling question: " D–do they h–have schools in Canada, sir?"

The schoolboy who dreams of the perfect country without schools had better not come to Canada. Canada has lots of schools of many different kinds, shapes, and sizes.

As in Britain there are two main types of schools: those supported independently by fees and those supported by the taxpayer. To confuse the Englishman the government schools are called Public schools; the independent schools are called Private. The main difference in the two types of schools is that the Public schools are "co-educational" and the private schools are either for boys or girls. Of these private or independent schools by far the most numerous are those of the Roman Catholic Church which are known as "separate schools". The arrangements governing their establishment and operation varies from province to province, but in the main they are operated quite independently within the general scheme of forms and examinations of the particular province. They are run by the Church and the teachers for the most part are priests and sisters. The subjects taught are of course the subjects of other schools but obviously since they are church schools they have a more strongly religious side to them than in the ordinary non-denominational government schools. The right of the Roman Catholic Church to establish its own schools dates back to the days of the fall of New France when certain privileges of religion, language, law, and education were granted to French Canadians.

Of the other independent schools in Canada little need be said here, beyond mentioning the fact of their existence. There are very few of them in proportion to the population compared with Britain. On the whole both the boys' and girls' schools are fashioned after their British counterparts with obvious modifications to suit another country and another people. They are for the most part boarding or boarding and day schools and attempt, as do their British brothers and sisters, to provide for their pupils a wider and more "all-round" education than is perhaps possible in most publicly owned and operated schools.

We have noticed a few of the many problems which arise in a country with as thinly sprinkled a population as Canada. Not the least of these is the teaching of "reading, writing, and 'rithmetic'" to small and scattered groups of children in outlying and sometimes very remote districts. There are a tremendous number of single room "little red school houses" in Canada where a teacher, with scant equipment and little money, copes with ten to thirty children, ranging in age perhaps from six to sixteen. Very often the teacher is also caretaker of the school and manages in his or her "spare" time to organise games and other activities for the pupils. Very often, too, the children coming from such schools into universities in various parts of the country, find that the unselfish devotion of their local teacher to the fundamentals of early education has prepared them admirably for more senior work. Without such teachers the education of young Canadians would collapse. To these small country schools children often come from considerable distances in all weathers and by many different means. School buses are used to collect the youngsters in some places but in others, where the country is too rough for wheeled transport, children may have to walk or ride a horse several miles each day. Some families are so isolated— so far away from other families—that there is no possibility of the children attending school, and in these cases the various provincial departments of education teach their scattered students by correspondence.

Every province in Canada has at least one University and in some there are several. Like the schools these universities are of two kinds: those supported by the provinces themselves and those supported privately. They vary greatly in size and to some extent in quality, but collectively and individually they have achieved great things for the country. In the dramatic field of scientific, engineering, and medical research certain of the universities have achieved world-wide recognition. In the less spectacular job of teaching young Canadians—helping them to lead more interesting lives and fitting them to earn their living, they have done, and are doing, a good job.

From all that has been said the reader will rightly conclude that there is no very striking difference between British and Canadian education; and yet perhaps there is one big difference. It is a difference more of holiday activity than of school activity. In Canada school runs from the first week in September to the last week in June with about two weeks off at Christmas-time and a week or ten days at Easter. Universities begin their work at the end of September and finish before the middle of May, with only short Christmas and Easter holidays. During this two month summer holiday for school children and almost five month holiday for university students, the great majority of the boys and many of the girls over the age of fourteen or fifteen, find jobs which keep them busy for the summer months. The younger ones may caddy at golf courses, act as errand boys; girls work in shops, act as gardeners' helpers or anything else for which they are physically and mentally able. University students, many of whom rely on this summer money to pay for their winter education, find work on construction gangs, as waitresses in summer hotels, in factories, in offices, on survey gangs or in any of a hundred and one other occupations. This early experience of hard work in a paid job generally tends to make

Canadian boys and girls practical and confident of their ability to earn their living.

One thing, however, should be clearly understood. Even though a Canadian boy may be going to join a road gang the day after he finishes school for the year; even though his school day may be only five hours long and the work easy, whereas he will soon be shovelling gravel for eight hours in the hot sun; even though his teachers at school are kind and the foreman of the road gang tough; the Canadian schoolboy like his British brother looks forward with unconcealed eagerness to the summer holidays, and after geometry, algebra, history, chemistry, and all the rest, shovelling gravel *is* a holiday.

XII

CANADIANS AT WORK

THE growth and development of Canada has been rapid and exciting. We have seen something of the speed with which log cabin settlements in the forest have mushroomed into thriving modern cities and of how huge distances have been spanned by road and rail. In the space of what historians would call only a few years, Canada has grown from a colony, dependent on furs and fish, to an independent dominion of both agricultural and industrial strength. All this has been the result partly of fertile plains, wide timber lands, abundant raw materials, and in general the richness and variety of the country itself, but it has also been brought about by long hours of hard work both mental and physical. Canadians are a happy and hard working people. They have worked and are working to good effect.

In the early part of the nineteenth century trapping began to give way to lumbering and agriculture began to claim an increasingly important place in the pattern of Canadian life. Now, a little over a hundred years later, agriculture in its many forms is the country's most important single industry. Of all the men gainfully employed in Canada nearly a third of them are employed in occupations directly concerned with agriculture. On the great plains of the western provinces and under the broad sunny skies of this land, crops of many kinds ripen and are harvested each year.

The number of acres devoted to five of the field crops—wheat, oats, barley, rye, and flax are almost equal to the combined areas of England and Scotland. The growing of these crops has never been easy and has frequently proved to be a heart-breaking business. There is one thing that is sure about farming in the West and that is that nothing *is* sure. There have been wonderful years when a great demand for Canadian wheat coincided with a big yield of good grain, but there have been years when thousands upon thousands of bushels were ploughed back into the fields, or left to rot in storage because there was too much grain and not enough buyers for it. Nearly every year some farmers in some districts see their crop beaten to the ground by hail before it can be harvested, and often an early winter may cover the unreaped grain with snow. There have been years of drought and years of too much rain; there have been years of grasshopper plagues.

One year, after a grasshopper plague had devastated many thousands of acres in southern Saskatchewan, a great many farmers in the area received an advertisement for a "sure grasshopper killer". They were advised to send one dollar to a given address for which they would receive the "killer" and complete instructions for its use. Many of them eagerly sent off their money and in time found themselves in receipt of a small package labelled "Do not open until grasshopper season." The following summer when the destructive insects returned in their millions the various farmers eagerly opened their little packages. What they found inside was a small wooden block labelled

"A" and a tiny wooden mallet labelled "B". The
instructions read: "Place grasshopper on block
'A' and strike with mallet 'B'."

But each year, in spite of difficulties, a combination of rich black earth and hard work produces
millions of bushels of wheat and the picture of
golden grain waving under a blue and cloudless
sky has become symbolic of western Canada.

In addition to field crops of many kind, from
wheat to sugar-beet, Canada produces cattle,
sheep, pigs, and poultry in vast quantities; it
produces many millions of dollars' worth of a
variety of fruits including some of the world's
finest apples. Canadian wine made from Canadian
grapes is pleasant and inexpensive. The national
tree, the maple, produces some two and a half
million gallons of its incomparable syrup each year,
and for those who persist in thinking of Canada as
a frozen wilderness, it may come as something of a
surprise to learn that tobacco growing is becoming
an increasingly important industry.

Canada is used to large scale operations but in
no industry is that more apparent than in the
production of lumber, pulp, and paper. More than
a third of the total land area of the country is
still covered with forest and of this an area about
twice the size of France is accessible for the cutting
and processing of timber. Timber is just as much a
crop as wheat. The only difference in the two
crops is that wheat takes only a summer to reach
maturity whereas trees take a number of years.
The millions upon millions of dollars' worth of
trees which are harvested each year must be replaced
if future generations are going to reap a similar

EARLY MORNING IN THE WEST : LOADING THE HORSES

side of the Atlantic than on the east, and provide better and fuller lives for themselves and their families. They have found both food and work plentiful and varied, and they have also discovered that higher pay is matched if not quite cancelled out by a higher cost of living. They have discovered too, those who have found their way into industry, that Canadian workers are protected by the same unions and machinery for collective bargaining that safeguard the workers of the older countries. Most of the local trade unions in Canada are branches of international organisations with headquarters in the United States.

It is never easy to speak confidently of particular national characteristics which distinguish the men of one country from those of another. There is no such person as a typical Canadian. One characteristic which most Canadians share, however, is a tremendous belief in the future of their country. Canadians, as a race, are cheerful optimists. They are inclined to believe that however good life is to-day it is going to be even better to-morrow, and it is with that confidence of a happy future that Canadians go to work to-day.

F

XIII

CANADIANS AT PLAY

ONE need not travel far from any Canadian city or town to reach fairly wild country. Half a day's journey at the most by car will take one into areas which, if not quite uncivilised, are at any rate almost unpopulated. It is to and through such areas that thousands of Canadians travel each year, and so many and so large are these areas that except for fashionable resorts here and there they remain unspoiled and uncrowded. The attractions of these unpeopled stretches of country are almost irresistible to all but the most confirmed city dweller. A Toronto boy living the winter round in this big, industrial city can set off with a friend on the morning of the first day of the summer holidays and by evening be frying his sizzling bacon over a crackling camp fire, his canoe pulled up on the shore, his tent set back among the wind-bent pines, and the pure cold lake water lapping against the rocks. His friend can be fishing nearby for a black bass to go with the bacon. Toronto may be only a hundred miles away, but it might be ten thousand. To the Ontario boy a canoe trip is the most obvious way of spending a holiday, and the northern Ontario country with its chains of crystal-clear lakes, its pines and rocks and birds, animals, and fish is the best country in the world for a canoe and a boy.

The Canadian countryside is free. There are few private hunting or fishing rights. The laws which control such sports are the laws of government and, subject to the limits of size and catch which protect the wild creatures, any man may, when the season comes, buy a licence and set out into the wilds in search of big game, bird, or fish.

The country itself is the greatest single attraction for Canadians after work is done and before it begins again. The sports of this country—camping, hiking, canoeing, climbing, fishing, hunting, ski-ing, and a hundred more are Canada's "natural" sports, but like every other country Canada is enthusiastic about the sport of games and particularly hockey. Just as the British youngster, almost as soon as he learns to walk, begins to kick things about in preparation for football, so the Canadian child, wherever there is ice, is given a pair of skates and encouraged to slither about in anticipation of hockey games ahead. Sometimes the unsteady infant pushes a wooden chair before him to give him the support of six legs instead of two, but he soon discards this and staggers manfully about on his ankles, occasionally sitting down very suddenly, but persisting always. The result of all this is that in most parts of Canada hockey is a game nearly everyone has played and knows something about. Local hockey teams receive tremendous encouragement and support, and the fortunes of the big professional teams—and in particular the Toronto Maple Leafs—who play against American teams (frequently made up largely of Canadians) are followed right across the country. In Canada one never distinguishes between two games by calling one of them ice hockey. There is only one hockey.

After hockey comes rugby, which resembles the

British game in little more than the shape of the
ball used. Englishmen who do not understand the
game are always somewhat amazed at the shoulder
guards, helmets, and padding which the players
wear. In spite of all this protective clothing,
Canadian rugby is a tough bodily contact game
played with tremendous enthusiasm by schoolboys,
university students, and professional teams. The
biggest national sporting event in the country is
the annual rugby game between the top professional
teams of East and West.

The influence of American sport on that of
Canada has been great and although "soccer"
football, cricket, and rugger find enthusiastic players
in Canada they are not Canadian sports. The first
of these three is played after a fashion by a fair
number of boys and men, but the last two are
understood and played by a mere handful of people.
Of the countless other games and sports, both team
and individual, which are popular among Canadians,
no special mention need be made here. They are
equally well known on both sides of the Atlantic.
It may be well to point out, however, that Canada
has a national game—the old Indian game of
lacrosse. It is no longer widely popular throughout
the country, but where it is played it is as rugged
and hard fought a game, if not quite as ruthlessly
dangerous, as it was when the redskins once played
it in the forest clearing.

The social side of Canadian life, as opposed to
the working or business side, appears to the
European, like many other sides of Canada, to
be more American than British. Possibly Canadians
are inclined to open their hearts and homes to

new acquaintances more readily than are English-men—at least that is the common belief in Britain. If there is some truth in this it is very easy to exaggerate it. Canadian service men in Britain could not have been more hospitably received than they were. Many of them who had been brought up to believe that the Englishman or Scot is an aloof being who does not take kindly to outsiders, had their beliefs shattered by receiving more invitations than they could possibly accept. Canada being a country of many races and of a small population, its inhabitants are perhaps more curious and eager for knowledge about people of other lands. Perhaps too the spirit of the early days of settlement lingers on and there is a desire to make new arrivals feel at home in a new country

XIV

CANADA AND THE WORLD

CANADA is a large country with a small population. It has, as things are counted to-day, a small air force, a small army, and a small navy. It could not alone defend itself from attack. Yet in the world to-day Canada is in a position of tremendous importance, and perhaps the very word "position" is the word which explains it.

The land mass known as North America is divided by artificial lines into various countries. The line which divides Canada from the United States of America is in fact so unreal that in many places it simply does not exist except as a dotted line on a map. It has no natural or geographical basis at all. Canadians and Americans cross freely and with an absolute minimum of formality from one country into the other. American licence plates from every state in the union are no cause for comment in Canada and the Stars and Stripes often flies side by side with the Union Jack over Canadian hotels.

This free interchange of peoples and ideas has had a far more profound effect on Canada than it has on the United States. Canada is not a strong enough country to have much influence on Americans, but the wealth and power of the United States has had a very great influence on Canadian life. A broad river of manufactured goods, magazines, films, radio programmes, ideas, and people flows northwards flooding the whole country of Canada.

The result, as one might guess, is that in many ways Canadians speak and think like Americans. They are reading the same magazines, seeing the same movies, listening to the same radio programmes, driving the same cars, and bringing up their children in the same sort of towns and cities with many of the same ideas. And beyond this Canada depends on the United States to protect her, for she knows that the United States *must* protect her in order to protect itself. Efficient and well-equipped as the Canadian forces may be, they would be inadequate if the safety of the land was really threatened. Economically, too, Canada and the States are drawn into a close partnership. Canada with its abundance of raw material is the ideal neighbour for the most highly industrialised country in the world.

But despite this interchange, Canada and the United States are two quite separate countries. Traditionally and constitutionally Canada is British. With the same Queen, the same form of government, the same organization of the armed forces, and with a great many descendants of people who deliberately chose British rule rather than American independence, Canada feels a strong pull to the east across the Atlantic Ocean. Sometimes British visitors to Canada are surprised at the display of loyalty to the British connection. The reason is not hard to find. Canada values its ties with the British Commonwealth, but they are ties which, formed as they are of strands of sentiment and tradition, might give way eventually before the tremendous counter-pull from the south. Thus it is that Canadians work consciously to preserve and strengthen these bonds. Canada has no desire to revert to the position of a colony in the British Empire, but neither does she wish to find herself absorbed by the United States. Canada wishes to remain as she is—a free and independent country thinking and acting for herself.

Canada, half British, half American, finds herself in a unique and vitally important position. It is her job to act as an interpreter. More than any other people in the world Canadians are fitted to explain Britons to Americans and Americans to Britons. It is the job of the Canadian to assure the Englishman that all Americans are not loud and boastful and to convince the American that all Englishmen are not snobs obsessed with feudal notions of class distinction. They must do this job not merely on an individual level, they must do it internationally. Such a role is not an easy one. It is difficult to be a really good interpreter and retain a distinct personality of one's own. The danger of the Canadian position is that she may fail to develop a distinctively Canadian outlook. John Bull is known across the world as the personification of Britain, and Uncle Sam is a well-known representation of the United States, but few people recognise the tough man in shirt sleeves called Jack Canuck. He is intended to stand for Canada, but his personality is vague. There is some thought that the personality of the country itself may be vague likewise.

Since the last war Canada has taken a greater part in world affairs than ever before, and the personality of the country is beginning to be felt in the councils of nations. What is this personality?

What does Canada stand for? Has Canada anything we might call a foreign policy?

Let us say first of all that, in a world where the
man with the biggest muscles often has the biggest
say in affairs, Canada's muscles do not enable her
to dictate and enforce her ideas by threat of violence.
The strength of the country rests then, not on
atomic bombs, but on ideas and ideals. Canada
has been close enough to Europe in two devastating
wars to have a fairly clear first-hand knowledge
of the misery which many Europeans have endured.
On the other hand, Canadians have grown up in a
spacious land of peace, security, and good food.
The hardships and calamities which many Europeans have been forced to endure has tended to
make them cynical and doubtful of confident
promises of "better times just around the corner".
Canadians by comparison are idealists. They
would genuinely like to see others as happy and
well fed as themselves. Between the wars and since
the last war they have welcomed thousands of
immigrants to their country. They have found
them work and given them a start in the New World.
But Canadians know that no matter how open their
immigration policy, the difficulties of Europe are
not going to be solved by allowing some Europeans
to come to live in Canada. They know too that
to admit too many at one time would give rise to
difficult problems within the country. Canadian
foreign policy, then, is genuinely one of helping
not only to maintain peace but of helping to improve
the lot of poorer and more crowded nations. She
has her own ideas as to how this end may be
achieved. Sometimes her ideas are also those of

Britain; sometimes they are those of the United States; sometimes they are shared by many countries; sometimes by only a few. The important thing is that whether shared by others or not, they are Canada's ideas, just as much as they are America's, Britain's, France's, Australia's or anyone else's ideas. Canada is no longer a mirror reflecting British or American policy. She is developing a separate policy of her own.

Like the United States, Canada has admitted peoples of many different races. These new arrivals, however, do not seem to become Canadians as quickly as new arrivals to the south become Americans, and in many of the so-called "foreign" districts men and women from central Europe continue for years to speak their own languages and cling as far as possible to the way of life they knew in Europe. It is not unusual to stop for a drink of water at a farmhouse in Alberta and find the farmer unable to understand even simple English. Sometimes even the children speak only the faltering English of their schoolroom for it is only in the schoolroom that they speak it at all. The Canadian government is very aware of this problem of converting the people of many nationalities into Canadians, and is doing a great deal to help and encourage these new Canadians to become so in more than name. It is not a task which will be accomplished in a few weeks or months, but once it is achieved Canada will draw new strength from such people. The first-hand knowledge of Europe which they bring with them, and the collective working out of their problems in a new country, is of great value to Canada in her dealings with Europe and her understanding of other lands.

Canada has in years past welcomed people of many countries and has given them a chance to work hard and to make their own opportunities. In time to come others will follow; some to visit and some to stay. In this book some attempt has been made to show such visitors what they may expect to see and how Canada has grown up. The visitor to Canada will see much that has been done; he will see much that is being done; and he will see much that is yet to be done. It is this last sight which should prove the most exciting. In many older countries one may feel that development has gone almost as far as it can go; one may feel that there are too many people and too few new opportunities. In Canada conditions are the exact opposite. The development has just begun. Far from being over-crowded, Canadian towns and cities still speak proudly of increases in population and there are still thousands of square miles of country waiting for the future.

APPENDIX

GOVERNMENT

The Governor General is the Queen's representative in Canada. He is appointed by the Queen on the advice of the Canadian Government. The Present Governor General is the first Canadian to be appointed to the post.

The Cabinet is chosen in the same way as the British Cabinet.

Parliament. The Canadian House of Commons is made up of some 260 members. The two largest political parties in Canada are the Liberals and Conservatives. Other parties are the Co-operative Commonwealth Federation (C.C.F.) and the Social Credit.

The Senate is roughly equivalent to the British House of Lords. Its members are appointed by the government in power and hold their seats for life.

Provincial Government is similar to Dominion Government on a smaller scale. Members of the ten provincial parliaments are called either M.P.P. (Member Provincial Parliament) or M.L.A. (Member Legislative Assembly). The Lieutenant Governor, appointed by the Dominion Government, is the Queen's representative in the province.

POPULATION

The total population according to the 1951 census was 14,009,429.

The population by racial origin in 1951 was as follows:

English	3,630,344
Irish	1,439,635
Scottish	1,547,470
Other British	92,236
French	4,319,167
German	619,995
Scandinavian	283,024
Ukranian	395,043
Polish	219,845
Jewish	181,670
Netherlands	264,267
Russian	91,279
Italian	152,245
Austrian	32,231
Belgian	35,148
Czech, Slovak	63,959
Finnish	43,745
Hungarian	60,460
Rumanian	23,601
Other European Races	87,210
Chinese	32,528
Japanese	21,663
Other Asiatic Races	18,636
Indians, Eskimos	165,607
Negroes	18,020
Others	170,401

APPENDIX 83

RELIGION

The number of adherents to each of the main churches in 1951 were:

Roman Catholic	6,070,000
United Church of Canada	2,867,000
Church of England in Canada	2,061,000
Presbyterian	782,000
Baptist	520,000
Lutheran	445,000

Religions, however, are as diversified as the population. There are at least thirty religions each claiming membership of 10,000 or more.

IMPORTS AND EXPORTS

Imported from British Commonwealth countries in 1957 goods worth $760,818,893.

Exported to British Commonwealth countries in 1957 goods worth $970,647,627.

Imported from Foreign countries in 1957 goods worth $4,862,591,566.

Exported to Foreign countries in 1957 goods worth $3,870,081,731.

Imported from U.S.A. in 1957 goods worth $3,998,549,364.

Exported to U.S.A. in 1957 goods worth $2,869,247,048.

Canada had export and import dealings with about 160 different countries in 1957.

NATIONAL ANTHEM

"God Save the Queen" is played, as in Britain, on official occasions and at the beginning or end of theatrical performances, etc. Canada's own national anthem "O Canada" is often used also on such occasions. Below is the first verse in English and in French:

O Canada!
Our home and native land,
True patriot love in all thy sons command.
With glowing hearts we see thee rise,
The true North, strong and free;
And stand on guard,
O Canada, Stand aye on guard for thee.

O Canada!
Terre de nos aïeux,
Ton front est ceint de fleurons glorieux!
Car ton bras sait porter l'épée
Il sait porter la croix:
Ton histoire est une épopée
Des plus brillants exploits.

CURRENCY

Monetary unit—the Canadian dollar, which is worth about 7s.

POPULATION OF LARGEST TOWNS (1951 census)

Montreal	1,021,520
Toronto	675,754
Vancouver	344,833
Winnipeg	235,710
Hamilton	208,321
Ottawa	202,045
Quebec	164,016
Windsor	120,049

AREAS OF THE GREAT LAKES

	sq. miles
Lake Superior	31,820
Lake Michigan	22,400
Lake Huron	23,010
Lake St. Clair	460
Lake Erie	9,940
Lake Ontario	7,540

PROVINCES AND THEIR CAPITALS

Newfoundland	St. John's
Prince Edward Island	Charlotte-town
Nova Scotia	Halifax
New Brunswick	Fredericton
Quebec	Quebec City
Ontario	Toronto
Manitoba	Winnipeg
Saskatchewan	Regina
Alberta	Edmonton
British Columbia	Victoria

LEADING INDUSTRIES

Vegetable products
Animal products
Textiles and textile products
Wood and paper products
Iron and its products
Non-ferrous metal products
Non-metallic mineral products
Chemicals and allied products

TIME ZONES

Atlantic time
Eastern time
Central time
Mountain time
Pacific time

INDEX

(Items contained in the Appendix are not indexed)